Cambridge Experience Readers

Level 1

Series editor: Nich

Harry's Holiday

Antoinette Moses

CAMBRIDGE

CAMBRIDGE
UNIVERSITY PRESS

c/ Orense, 4 - 13°, 28020 Madrid, Spain

Cambridge University Press is part of the University of Cambridge.

It furthers the University's mission by disseminating knowledge in the pursuit of education, learning and research at the highest international levels of excellence.

www.cambridge.org
Information on this title: www.cambridge.org/9788483238356

First published 2011
4th printing 2014

Antoinette Moses has asserted her right to be identified as the Author of the Work in accordance with the Copyright, Design and Patents Act 1988.

ISBN 978-84-8323-835-6 Paperback; legal deposit: M-25361-2011

No character in this work is based on any person living or dead.
Any resemblance to an actual person or situation is purely accidental.

Illustrations by Mikela Prevost

Editorial management, exercises and audio recordings by hyphen S.A.

Cover design by Zoográfico

Cambridge University Press has no responsibility for the persistence or accuracy of URLs for external or third-party internet websites referred to in this publication, and does not guarantee that any content on such websites is, or will remain, accurate or appropriate. Information regarding prices, travel timetables, and other factual information given in this work is correct at the time of first printing but Cambridge University Press does not guarantee the accuracy of such information thereafter.

Contents

People in the story

Harry Archer: a thirteen-year-old boy
Mrs Archer: Harry's mother
Tom: Harry's best friend
Zoe: Harry's friend
Mr Francis: Harry's English teacher
Lizzie: this woman works for Your Dream Holiday
Mrs Swann: the head teacher at Harry's school
Peter: this man works for Arsenal football team

BEFORE YOU READ

 Look at the pictures in Chapter 1. Answer the questions.

1 What is Harry looking at in the photo?

....

2 What do Harry and his mum watch on TV?

....

We're a team

'Here, Mum,' said Harry. 'Here's a cup of tea.'

'Thanks, Harry,' said his mother.

Harry Archer watched his mother. Her hands were bad today, he thought. He helped her take the cup. She was always bad on cold days. And this April was very cold.

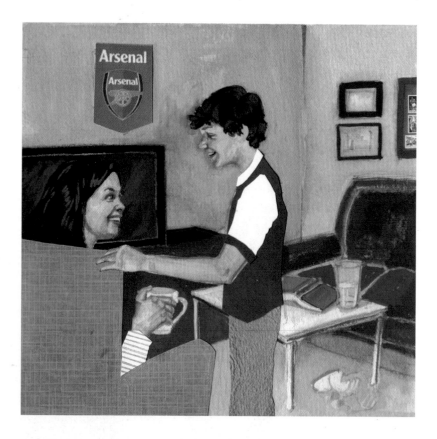

'Are you OK now?' Harry, asked. 'Do you need the bathroom?'

'No, I'm fine, Harry,' said Mrs Archer. 'Come and sit down. The football is starting in five minutes.'

'Yeah,' said Harry. 'And it's a big game. Arsenal against Chelsea. I can't wait!'

Mrs Archer laughed. 'You're just like your dad. When you were a baby, your first word …'

'… was football,' said Harry. 'I know, Mum!'

'Your dad laughed and laughed.' His mother smiled. Harry smiled too.

He thought about his father. 'Do you think Dad is watching this game?' he asked.

'Of course he is. He's an Arsenal fan[1], like you,' his mum replied. 'He always watches his favourite team.'

'Where is he today?' Harry asked. He looked at the photo on the wall of his dad next to a ship.

'Lagos, Nigeria,' said his mother. 'They're leaving on the ship today.'

'Hmm,' thought Harry. He looked out of the window. 'It isn't raining and cold in Nigeria.'

'He's going to be home for Christmas this year,' his mother told him.

'That's great,' said Harry. 'It isn't easy without Dad.'

'No,' replied his mother. 'It's hard for you. But I can't …' She stopped and looked down at her hands. Harry didn't say anything.

'It's all right, Mum,' said Harry quickly. 'We're fine, you and me.'

'But it isn't all right,' she replied. 'You don't do things that other teenagers do.'

'They don't do anything interesting,' said Harry.

'But other teenagers play football, talk to their friends, go shopping and other things. You're always at home. 'It's Saturday today, there's a big game, and you're here watching it with me.'

'It's OK,' said Harry. 'I don't need a football ticket. It's a lot of money.'

'I know,' said his mum, 'Perhaps you can stop eating chocolate for a month to get the money for a ticket?'

Harry laughed. 'I don't know, Mum … a month is a long time!'

'I know it's hard for you,' said his mum. 'But when my arthritis is bad, I can't do anything.'

'And that's why Mrs Stevens comes here,' said Harry.

'Yes,' said his mum. 'Mrs Stevens cleans the kitchen and the bathroom, but she doesn't buy food or cook. You do all that. And you do everything at the weekends.'

'Mum, it's all right,' said Harry. 'We're OK, you and me. We're a team.'

'Yes, but I often think about all the things you can't do,' his mum replied. 'You can't play football after school. You can't go to the cinema. You can't—'

'Shh, Mum,' said Harry. 'The football is starting ...'

Twenty minutes later, Chelsea got a goal. Arsenal 0 Chelsea 1.

'One goal is OK,' said his mother. 'Arsenal are going to win this game. I know it.'

She looked over at Harry. His eyes were almost closed. He was tired.

LOOKING BACK

●●

1 Check your answers to *Before you read* on page 4.

ACTIVITIES

●●

2 Complete the sentences with the names in the box.

> Harry's dad (x 2)   Harry (x 3)
>
> Harry's mum (x 2)   Mrs Stevens

1 ....*Harry*........ gives his mum a cup of tea.
2 .... is never good when it's cold.
3 The first word .... said was football.
4 .... is on a ship in Nigeria.
5 .... is going to be at home at Christmas.
6 .... can't do anything when her arthritis is bad.
7 .... comes to the house to clean.
8 .... is very tired.

3 Underline the correct words in each sentence.

1 Harry helps his mum take the cup of *tea* / *coffee*.
2 The football game on TV is starting in *five* / *ten* minutes.
3 Arsenal are playing *Manchester United* / *Chelsea*.
4 There is a photo of Harry's dad next to a *car* / *ship*.
5 Harry is at home with his *mum* / *dad* on Saturday.
6 Harry says other *teenagers do* / *don't do* interesting things.
7 Mrs Stevens cleans the *bedrooms* / *kitchen*.

4 Who or what do the <u>underlined</u> words refer to?

> Harry's dad   a football ticket   Harry's mum
> Harry (x 2)   Mrs Stevens   Harry and Harry's mum

1 He helped <u>her</u> take the cup. (page 5) ....*Harry's mum*....

2 '<u>You</u>'re just like your dad. (page 6) ....

3 '<u>He</u>'s an Arsenal fan.' (page 7) ....

4 <u>She</u> doesn't buy food or cook. (page 8) ....

5 '<u>It</u>'s a lot of money.' (page 8) ....

6 '<u>We</u>'re a team.' (page 9) ....

7 <u>He</u> was tired. (page 9) ....

5 Match the questions with the answers.

1 What are Harry and his mum going to watch on TV? [a]

2 What is Harry and his dad's favourite football team? ☐

3 When is Harry's dad going to be home? ☐

4 Who buys and cooks the food? ☐

a Football.

b Harry.

c Arsenal.

d Christmas.

LOOKING FORWARD

6 Tick (✓) what you think happens in Chapters 2 and 3.

1 Harry wants to win a holiday for his mum and dad. ☐

2 Harry plays football after school and doesn't look after his mum. ☐

Chapter 2

The competition

It was Wednesday morning and Harry and his best friend Tom were in their classroom.

'And Harry Archer runs up to the ball and he kicks it and —' Tom shouted.

As Harry kicked the ball to Tom their English teacher Mr Francis walked in and caught it.

'Well done, Mr Francis,' said Tom.

'No balls in the classroom, Harry,' said Mr Francis. 'You know that.'

'Sorry, Mr Francis,' said Harry.

'You can play football at break, lunchtime and after school,' said Mr Francis, 'but not in the classroom.'

'Harry never plays football after school,' said Zoe and laughed.

Harry's face went red. Everyone in the class knew that he was different[2]. He went home after school and didn't play with them, or go out. But only Tom knew the reason. He didn't want everyone else to know.

'Shh!' Tom told Zoe.

After class, Zoe went up to Harry and said sorry. Harry knew that Zoe's family had problems too. Her family lived in Harry's street. He sometimes saw a police car in front of their house.

'That's OK, Zoe,' said Harry.

'I've got a football magazine,' said Zoe. 'It's my brother's. Do you want to read it?' She gave it to Harry.

'Hey, thanks, Zoe,' said Harry and he took the magazine.

Zoe liked Harry. He had a nice smile. He was smiling now, with the magazine in his hand. Zoe smiled too and left the room.

'Zoe likes you,' laughed Tom.

'Don't be stupid,' said Harry.

Tom took the magazine. 'Look, there's a picture of Arsenal here.' Then he stopped.

'Hey, Harry,' he said. 'Look at this advert. It's a competition[3]. It says that you can win a holiday in Spain and it's easy. You never have a holiday.'

Harry didn't reply.

'We're going to go to Brighton this year,' said Tom. 'My uncle's got a hotel there. They've got lots of rooms at the hotel. I can talk to Dad. You can come too.'

'I can't,' said Harry. 'I can't leave Mum.'

'Of course,' said Tom. 'Sorry. You can't leave your mum. But … she can go to Spain! With you!'

'Hot weather is good for people with arthritis,' said Harry.

'So you must win this holiday,' said Tom.

Harry looked at the advert.

'Write five hundred words about why you want a holiday,' he read, 'and send it to Your Dream[4] Holiday.'

'You're good at writing stories,' said Tom.

Harry smiled. 'I'm going to do it. I'm going to win the holiday. We can all go to Spain. Mum and Dad are going to sit in the sun and we're all going to have a holiday!'

Chapter 3

Five hundred words

The next day Harry told his friends about the competition.

'I'm going to write five hundred words,' he said.

A boy called Sam laughed. 'I know five hundred words,' he said.

'Yes,' said Tom, 'and they're all bad words!'

Everyone laughed.

'Why do you want to win a holiday, Harry?' Zoe asked. Harry opened his mouth. He wanted to say, 'The holiday is for my mum', but he didn't.

'That's the competition question,' said Tom.

'Yes,' said Harry quickly.

'How do you win?' Zoe asked.

'I write five hundred words and say why I want this holiday,' said Harry. He stopped and thought.

'Why do you want to win?' Zoe asked again.

'I want to go to Spain because ...' He stopped again. He didn't want to tell his friends about his mum.

'I want to go to Spain because it's raining today,' said Zoe.

'I want to go to Spain because we have Maths today,' said Sam.

'I want to go to Spain because it's a free[5] holiday!' said Tom.

'Great,' said Harry, and he laughed. 'Thanks everyone.'

That evening Harry sat in his room at home and started writing:

I want to win this holiday because I never go on holiday. My dad works on a ship and my mum's got arthritis. After school, I look after[6] her and …

Harry stopped and read the first sentences again. 'This is boring,' he thought. He started again.

In a small room in a flat in London sits a woman. She doesn't want to sit in this flat. She wants to do things. She likes music and dancing. She loves cooking for her family. But she doesn't do these things because she's got arthritis. Her hands and feet and legs often hurt[7]. But she never talks about it.

This woman is my mother. She smiles all the time, but nothing is easy for her. I want her to laugh. I want her to have fun. And a holiday can do this for her.

You can get arthritis at any age. In the UK, 8.5 million people have got it. Some are like my mum and it's very bad. They feel tired all the time. Their arms, legs or hands hurt a lot. It never stops. Some days it's bad. On other days it's very bad.

'This is good,' thought Harry. But he also wanted to write about his mother before the arthritis. She worked in an office[8] then and she loved dancing. She smiled a lot. She was happy.

'Can I do this?' he thought. 'Can I win this holiday?' Harry started writing again.

LOOKING BACK

1 Check your answers to *Looking forward* on page 11.

ACTIVITIES

2 <u>Underline</u> the correct words in each sentence.

1 <u>Zoe</u> / *Tom* says that Harry never plays football after school.

2 Harry sometimes sees a *bus* / *police* car in front of Zoe's house.

3 There's a picture of *Chelsea* / *Arsenal* in the football magazine.

4 Tom is going to *Spain* / *Brighton* for his holiday this year.

5 *Sam* / *Tom* s ays he wants to go to Spain because it's a free holiday.

6 Harry writes five hundred words *at school* / *at home* for the competition.

7 Harry's mum loved *dancing* / *running* before the arthritis.

3 Put the sentences in order.

1 Zoe says sorry to Harry after class. ☐

2 Mr Francis catches the ball. ☐

3 Tom sees the holiday competition in the magazine. ☐

4 Harry starts writing five hundred words for the competition. ☐

5 Zoe gives Harry a football magazine. ☐

6 Tom says Zoe likes Harry. ☐

7 Harry tells Zoe and Sam about the competition. ☐

4 Are the sentences true (*T*) or false (*F*)?

1 Mr Francis says Harry and Tom can play football in the classroom. ☐*F*

2 Harry knows that Zoe's family have problems too. ☐

3 Zoe thinks Harry has a nice smile. ☐

4 Harry can go to Brighton with Tom. ☐

5 Tom says Harry is good at writing stories. ☐

6 Harry is going to write four hundred words for the competition. ☐

7 8.5 million people in the UK have got arthritis. ☐

8 Before the arthritis, Harry's mum worked in a shop. ☐

5 Answer the questions.

1 Why does Harry never play football after school?

....

2 Where has Tom's uncle got a hotel?

....

3 Why does Harry write five hundred words?

....

LOOKING FORWARD

● ●

6 Tick (✓) what you think happens in Chapters 4 and 5.

1 Harry's mum doesn't want a holiday in Spain. ☐

2 Harry gets a letter from Your Dream Holiday. ☐

Chapter 4

Harry won!

The next day Harry sent his letter to Your Dream Holiday. For two months, he heard nothing about the competition. There was a week's holiday from school. Arsenal lost in the FA Cup final against Liverpool. Teachers started talking about the end-of-year exams.

Then, one day in June, Harry got a letter. He ran into the kitchen with it.

'Mum!' shouted Harry, 'I've got a letter. It's from Your Dream Holiday. It's about the competition!'

'What competition?' asked his mother.

'It was a competition to win a holiday in Spain,' said Harry.

'You didn't tell me about that!' said his mother. 'Did you win?'

Harry opened the letter and smiled. 'Yes, I won!'

'Wow!' said Harry's mum. 'What does it say?'

Harry gave her the letter and she read it. 'This is great, Harry,' she said. 'But you can't go without Dad or me.'

'I know, Mum,' said Harry. 'I wanted to win the holiday for us – for you, me … and Dad if he can come.'

'Oh, Harry,' said his mum.

'And the holiday is free,' said Harry. 'We can sit in the sun and you can feel good again.'

'Thank you so much, Harry,' said his mother. 'I must tell your dad. He's going to be very happy.'

Harry ran to school.

'I won the competition!' he told Tom.

'Competition?' his friend replied.

'The holiday!' Harry shouted. 'In Spain!'

'Wow!' said Tom. He got onto his chair and shouted, 'Harry won!'

Mr Francis walked in and stopped.

'What are you doing, Tom?' he asked.

'Sorry, Mr Francis,' Tom said. He got off the chair. 'Harry won a free holiday. In a competition,' said Tom.

'Is this true?' asked Mr Francis.

'Yes,' said Harry. He told Mr Francis all about the competition. 'I wrote five hundred words,' he said. 'It was like an essay.'

'Wow, Harry,' said Mr Francis, smiling. 'You must read it to the class. We want to hear it.'

Harry had a copy of his competition essay in his bag, but he didn't want to read it to the class. He didn't want to tell everyone about his mum.

'I don't have it here,' Harry replied. 'It's at home.'

After class Harry walked over to Mr Francis's desk. He wanted to talk to him about his essay. He liked Mr Francis. 'He's going to understand,' thought Harry.

'Mr Francis,' Harry said. 'I don't want to read my competition essay to the class.'

'Why?' asked Mr Francis.

Harry took the essay out of his bag and gave it to his teacher. Mr Francis read about Harry's mother and her arthritis, and about the work that Harry does for her every day.

'I understand now, Harry,' said Mr Francis. 'It's a very good essay.'

'Thank you,' said Harry and gave him the letter from Your Dream Holiday.

'I need to go to this hotel in London on 22nd June. I need to get the tickets,' he told Mr Francis. 'It's in the centre of London. But 22nd June is a Friday. It's a school day.'

'Ah,' said Mr Francis.

'Can I go?' Harry asked him.

'I can ask the head teacher, Harry,' Mr Francis said, 'and you must also ask your mother.'

* * *

On 22nd June, it was sunny. Harry got up very early, dressed and had his breakfast.

'Good luck,' said his mum. She looked at her watch. 'You need to go. You're going to be late!' She smiled at Harry and he left the flat.

Harry walked to Finsbury Park – the Underground station near his flat. He took the Underground to Green

Park station and walked up the street to the hotel. It was a very big hotel and there were lots of people there. Harry spoke to the woman behind the desk.

'Hello. I'm here for the Your Dream Holiday competition,' he said.

'They're in the room over there on the left,' she replied.

Harry opened the door. The room was full of people.

'There are a hundred people in this room,' thought Harry. 'Why are there all these people here? Did they all win a holiday like me?'

Chapter 5

We all won!

Harry stood at the back of the room. There was a woman near him and he went up to her.

'Excuse me,' he said. 'Is this the room for Your Dream Holiday?'

'Yes,' she replied. 'Did you win?'

'Yes,' said Harry.

'I'm a winner[9] too' she said. 'Everyone here is a winner.'

'I don't understand,' said Harry.

'Come and sit down,' said the woman. 'They're going to tell us everything.'

Harry sat down. 'There are a hundred people in the room,' he thought. 'But a hundred free holidays is a lot of money. Why are there lots of winners?'

Then a door opened and a woman with a big smile walked into the room.

'Hello everybody,' she said. 'My name is Lizzie and I work for Your Dream Holiday. You're here today because you are all winners. Yes, you're all winners of a dream holiday in Spain!'

'Hooray!' shouted a man. Everybody laughed.

'This is great,' thought Harry. 'We're all going to get a free holiday.'

'Now,' said Lizzie. 'This is your hotel.' There was a picture behind her. It was of a very big hotel. 'It's next to the Mediterranean Sea and it's got three hundred rooms,' Lizzie told them. 'It's also got two swimming pools and a large garden.'

Harry thought about him and his mother in the hotel. 'Our garden is small. She's going to love the hotel's garden,' he thought. 'And she can sit next to the swimming pool and read.'

'It's a beautiful hotel,' said Lizzie. 'And all the food and drinks are free. You can eat and drink all day!'

'It looks great,' Harry said to the woman next to him.

'Yes,' she said, happily.

'Yes, it *looks* great, but is it all true?' said the man next to her.

'This is my husband,' said the woman. 'He doesn't think the holiday is going to be free,' she told Harry.

'They tell us that the food and drink are free,' said the man. 'But what about the other things?'

Lizzie smiled at everyone.

'Isn't it a beautiful hotel?' she said. 'It's very new. And we fly you to Spain from any London airport for free.'

'Excuse me,' the man said. He stood up. 'Is the hotel free?' he asked Lizzie.

Lizzie smiled. 'Well, we can't give everyone a week at a very expensive hotel.' She laughed. 'But we fly you to Spain and we pay[10] for all your meals and drinks at the hotel.'

'And the hotel?' the man asked again.

'Yes, you need to pay for the hotel,' said Lizzie very quickly. 'Of course you pay for the hotel.'

Then a woman at the front spoke. 'How much is it?' she asked.

'It isn't very expensive,' said Lizzie. 'There's a special price, just for winners of this competition.'

'We pay for the hotel?' said the woman beside Harry. She didn't look happy now.

'It *looks* like an expensive hotel,' said her husband. He stood up. 'It isn't a free holiday. This isn't a dream holiday,' he shouted at Lizzie. 'It's a *bad* dream!'

LOOKING BACK

● ●

① Check your answers to *Looking forward* on page 21.

ACTIVITIES

● ●

② <u>Underline</u> the correct words in each sentence.

1 Arsenal lose in the FA Cup final against *Chelsea /
   Liverpool.*

2 The letter from Your Dream Holiday says Harry
   won / didn't win the competition.

3 At school, Harry has his competition essay in his
   jacket / bag.

4 Harry goes to a hotel in *London / Brighton* to get the
   holiday tickets.

5 Harry takes the Underground to *Finsbury Park / Green
   Park.*

6 Lizzie says the *hotel / food* is free.

③ Complete the sentences with the words in the box.

garden	22nd June	Lizzie
for two months	chair	essay

1 Harry doesn't hear about the competition *for two months* .

2 Tom stands on a .... and shouts 'Harry won!'

3 Mr Francis says Harry's .... is very good.

4 Harry needs to go to London on ....

5 .... works for Your Dream Holiday.

6 The hotel has a ....

4 Match the two parts of the sentences.

1 What does Harry's letter from Your Dream Holiday say? [b]
2 Why doesn't Harry want to read his essay to the class? ☐
3 Why does Harry take the Underground on 22nd June? ☐
4 Why are all the people at the hotel? ☐
5 Why doesn't the woman next to Harry look happy? ☐

a Because he goes to a hotel in London to get the tickets.
b He won the competition.
c Because they're all winners.
d Because she must pay for the hotel.
e Because he doesn't want to tell everyone about his mum.

5 Answer the questions.

1 Why does Harry run into the kitchen?

....

2 What does Harry need to ask his mother?

....

3 What is going to be free at the hotel in Spain?

....

4 Why does the man shout at Lizzie?

....

LOOKING FORWARD
● ●

6 Tick (✓) what you think happens in the last three chapters.

1 Harry's dad comes home. ☐
2 Harry's mum gets a new carer[11]. ☐

Chapter 6

A bad dream

'This *is* a bad dream,' thought Harry. He sat in the chair in the hotel room. His mum and dad didn't have money for an expensive hotel.

He left the hotel and walked back to the station. 'I'm not a winner,' he thought. 'I didn't win anything.'

Harry walked into the flat and his mother knew that something was wrong.

'What is it?' she asked.

'I didn't win a free holiday,' said Harry. 'They don't pay for the hotel.' He told his mother about Lizzie and Your Dream Holiday.

'I'm sorry, Harry,' she said. 'Your Dream Holiday just used the competition to tell people about the hotel. I'm very sorry,' she said again.

Dudley Central Library

www.dudley.gov.uk/libraries
Tel: 01384 815560

Borrowed Items 04/02/2017 13.22
XXXXXXXX9360

m Title	Due Date
Blue Hen	04/03/2017
Harry's Holiday Level 1	04/03/2017
eginner/Elementary	

ndicates items borrowed today
hankyou for using this service

'What am I going to tell everyone at school?' asked Harry. 'They think I won a holiday.'

'Tell them everything,' said his mother.

'But I can't tell them why I wanted the holiday,' said Harry. 'I can't tell them about you and the arthritis and everything.'

'Your friends don't know about me?' asked his mother.

'They know I need to help at home a lot,' said Harry. 'They know you aren't always well. But they don't know why. Tom knows, but the others don't.'

'Then you're going to tell them,' said his mother. 'You look after me every day, and your friends need to know about it.'

Harry didn't say anything.

'Look, Harry,' said his mum. 'We're a great family. I love your dad and he loves me. He's got a good job and you're a great son. Your dad and I love you. Think about Zoe and her family. Zoe's mother comes to see me sometimes. They've got a lot of problems.'

At school on Monday, Harry told the class about Your Dream Holiday. But he didn't tell them about his mum.

'That isn't right,' said Tom. 'So they take you to Spain but you pay for the hotel?'

'Yes,' said Harry.

'I'm sorry, Harry,' said Mr Francis.

'It isn't right,' said Tom again. 'It isn't fair.'

Harry's friends were all angry. 'You must tell people about this,' said a boy called David.

'Yeah,' said a girl. 'Write about it, Harry.'

'That's a good idea,' said Tom. 'You can write about the competition on the school website. Then everyone in the world can read about it!'

'I don't know,' said Harry.

'I can write about it,' said Tom. 'Can I?' he asked Mr Francis.

'Ask Harry,' said Mr Francis.

Harry thought about his mum. She wanted his friends to know everything.

'Yes,' said Harry. 'Write about my mum. You can tell people why she needs a holiday.'

'Are you sure? Do you want Tom to write about it?' asked Mr Francis.

'Yes, I'm sure,' said Harry. He looked at the other students in the room. 'I know you all think I'm stupid because I'm always at home and I never go out after school. But my mum's not well. She's got arthritis and I look after her. I'm not stupid. I'm a carer.'

'Thank you, Harry,' said Mr Francis. 'I think we all understand that it isn't easy to tell us about your mother.

Being a carer is not easy. And you aren't stupid. We all know that.'

'Yeah,' said Zoe. She smiled at Harry and he smiled back at her.

'It's Your Dream Holiday that is stupid,' said Tom. 'But now everyone is going to know about them!'

Chapter 7

The school website

That night, Tom wrote about Harry and his mother. He worked for over two hours. In the morning he asked Harry to read it first. Harry liked it. Tom wrote well.

Then, in the afternoon, Tom saw Harry again.
'Fifty people visited the school website today!' he said.
The day after, they looked again. It was four hundred people. The day after that it was two thousand.

A week later, Mr Francis came into class and asked Harry to come to the office of the head teacher, Mrs Swann.

'Is it bad?' asked Harry.

'No,' said Mr Francis. 'Actually, it's very good. But Mrs Swann's going to tell you everything.'

They went into the office. Mrs Swann smiled at Harry.

'Hello, Harry,' she said. 'Do you see all this paper?'

Harry saw a lot of paper on Mrs Swann's desk.

'Yes,' he said.

'These are all emails for you,' she told him.

'Oh,' said Harry. 'I'm sorry.'

'It's all right,' she said and smiled. 'But you've got a lot of work to do. You must reply to all of them.'

Mrs Swann gave him one of the emails. It was from a girl in America.

'Hi, Harry,' he read. 'My name is Liana and I'm a carer too. My parents can't see and I do everything for them before and after school.'

He stopped reading and looked at Mrs Swann.

'There are lots of emails like this,' said Mrs Swann. 'And there are letters too.'

She gave him a letter and he opened it. 'Dear Harry,' the letter said. 'We are an organisation[12] called Young Carers and we read about you and your mother on your school website. We want you to write something for our website about your life as a young carer. We also have holidays for young carers and we want to give you a holiday this summer.'

'Young Carers want to give me a holiday,' Harry told Mrs Swann. 'But what about my mum?' he asked her.

'Now that everyone knows about your mother, things are going to change,' replied Mrs Swann. 'We're all going to help you.'

'Me?' asked Harry.

'Yes, you,' said Mrs Swann. 'Harry, there are lots of young carers in this country. But there is help for them. And at this school we're going to help you too.'

'Thank you,' said Harry.

'But there's one more email,' said Mrs Swann. 'It's from a holiday company. Not one like Your Dream Holiday. A good one this time. They want to give you *and* your family a holiday in Spain.'

'And it's free?' asked Harry.

'Yes,' said Mrs Swann. 'This time it's free.'

Chapter 8

Just wow!

Harry had the ball. The goal was just in front of him, but there was someone between him and the goal. There was a girl from his team next to him.

'Harry, Harry! Kick it to me! Here! Here!' she shouted.

Harry looked at the girl. He quickly kicked the ball to her and she kicked it into the goal.

'Goal!' shouted Harry. He and the girl jumped up and down happily.

'Well done, you two,' said the coach. 'That's good play.'

Harry smiled. 'I love this holiday,' he thought. All the kids were carers and it was so easy to talk to them. Everybody felt like a friend. Next week he and his mother and his father were all going to Spain. And his father had a new job in London.

'He's going to be living at home again,' thought Harry. 'It's wonderful. This is the best summer.'

*   *   *

Two months later and it was a new year at school. For Harry, everything was different. His father was at home again and his mother had a new carer. She came to their house in the morning and in the afternoon. She cleaned, she bought food from the shops and she made lunch for his mother too. Harry was in the school football team and on Saturdays he and his father watched Arsenal on the television.

Then, in October, Mrs Swann asked him to come to her office again.

'Hello, Harry,' she said. 'Come in. I want you to meet someone.'

There was a tall man in Mrs Swann's office. He looked friendly.

'Hi, Harry,' said the man. 'My name is Peter and I work for Arsenal football team.'

'Wow,' said Harry. 'Really?'

'Yes,' said Peter. 'We do lots of work with organisations that help people in London. And this year we're working with Young Carers. We're trying to help people like you, Harry.'

'That's great,' said Harry.

'But first we want you to help us,' said Peter.

'Me?' asked Harry.

'Yes,' said Peter. 'We want our fans to give money to organisations like Young Carers. We need someone to tell our fans about their work. We need someone like you.'

'But … how can I tell them?' said Harry. 'I don't know many people.'

'You can tell the fans about it at the game,' said Peter. 'On Saturday.'

'Me?' asked Harry.

'Yes you,' said Peter. 'And you can meet the Arsenal team too.'

'Me?' Harry asked again. 'Meet the team?'

'Is that OK?' asked Peter. 'Can you talk to the fans? Can you tell them about your work as a carer for your mother?'

Harry smiled. 'Yes,' he told Peter, 'It's OK. I want to tell them everything.'

'Great!' said Peter. He smiled too. 'And this is for you and your friend, Tom.'

He gave Harry an envelope.

*   *   *

'What?' shouted Tom. 'Harry, say that again! You're going to meet the Arsenal team this Saturday?'

'Yes,' laughed Harry, 'and there's also this ...'

He gave Tom the envelope. Tom opened it and his eyes grew very big.

'It's an Arsenal season ticket[13],' Tom said.

'No,' said Harry. 'There are *two* Arsenal season tickets. One is for you and one is for me!'

'Wow,' said Tom.

'Yeah,' said Harry. 'Just wow!'

LOOKING BACK

● ●

1 Check your answers to *Looking forward* on page 33.

ACTIVITIES

● ●

2 Put the sentences in order.

1 Harry's mum says his friends must know about her arthritis. ☐
2 Lots of people visit the school website. ☐
3 Harry's mum sees something is wrong with Harry. ☐*1*
4 Mrs Swann gives Harry a letter from Young Carers. ☐
5 Tom writes about Harry's mum on the school website. ☐
6 Harry and Tom get season tickets for Arsenal. ☐
7 Peter comes to Mrs Swann's office. ☐
8 A holiday company gives Harry and his parents a free holiday. ☐

3 Match the two parts of the sentences.

1 Why does Harry go to Mrs Swann's office? ☐*c*
2 Why does Liana send Harry an email? ☐
3 Why is Harry happier now? ☐
4 Why do Tom's eyes grow very big? ☐
5 What do Harry and his dad do on Saturdays? ☐

a Harry gives him an Arsenal season ticket.
b She's a carer too.
c She wants to give him the emails and letters.
d They watch Arsenal play football on TV.
e His dad is at home again and his mum has a new carer.

46

4 Are the sentences true (*T*) or false (*F*)?

1 Harry's mum and dad can pay for an expensive hotel. `F`

2 Zoe and her family have a lot of problems. ☐

3 Harry's friends are angry about the competition. ☐

4 Young Carers want to give Harry's mum and dad a holiday. ☐

5 Harry's dad gets a new job in London. ☐

6 Peter comes to Harry's classroom. ☐

7 Peter wants Harry to tell people about his work as a carer. ☐

8 There is one Arsenal season ticket in the envelope. ☐

 5 Underline the correct words in each sentence.

1 There are a lot of emails on Mrs Swann's *chair / desk.*

2 Liana lives in *Spain / America.*

3 Harry *hates / likes* his holiday with Young Carers.

4 Harry is going to meet the *Chelsea / Arsenal* team on Saturday.

6 Answer the questions.

1 What does Harry tell his friends at school?

....

2 How can everyone in the world read about Harry?

....

3 Where is Harry going to tell the Arsenal fans about his mother?

....

GLOSSARY

1 **fan** (page 7) *noun* someone who really likes a sports team

2 **different** (page 12) *adjective* not the same as somebody or something

3 **competition** (page 14) *noun* something a person tries to win

4 **dream** (page 15) *adjective* something you want very much

5 **free** (page 16) *adjective* when you don't need to give any money for something

6 **look after** (page 18) *verb* try to make sure somebody is well

7 **hurt** (page 19) *verb* when someone's body feels bad

8 **office** (page 19) *noun* a room where somebody works

9 **winner** (page 28) *noun* someone who wins a game or **competition**

10 **pay** (page 30) *verb* give money for something

11 **carer** (page 33) *noun* someone who **looks after** a person

12 **organisation** (page 40) *noun* a group of people who work together to help other people

13 **season ticket** (page 45) *noun* a ticket you can use many times e.g. to see a football game, but don't need to **pay** for each time